Tractatus Architectus in Two Hundred Tweets

Ganapathy Mahalingam

ISBN: 0692778306
ISBN-13: 978-0692778302 (Pensive Muse Books)

DEDICATION

Dedicated to all my teachers of Architecture, the ones I have met, and others who have inspired me through their remote presence.

CONTENTS

ACKNOWLEDGMENTS

My sincerest gratitude for the emergent possibility of melding
Wittgenstein and Twitter for a distillation of beliefs and
propositions arising from beliefs about Architecture

1 ARCHITECTURE

1.   Architecture is.

2.   Architecture is the art and science of building.

3.   Building is an act of putting things together.

4.   A thing is that which has been put together, a gathering of the material and the immaterial.

5.   Architecture is the putting together of building materials aesthetically to define the spaces we inhabit.

6.   In defining spaces, architectural assemblies have to resist natural forces such as gravity, wind, rain, snow, heat, and seismic forces.

7.   Architecture is an art because it enables lives to be lived.

8.   Thou art in Architecture.

9.   Good Architecture protects the health, safety, and welfare of the people whose lives it enables.

10.   Architecture is a science because it uses systems of knowledge to put a building together.

11. Architecture has to be imagined and designed before it is built.

12. Imagining Architecture involves multiple architectural senses.

13. Chief among the architectural senses is our visual sense. Another important architectural sense is our muscular or kinesthetic sense.

14. We use all our senses to experience Architecture.

15. We dwell in our architectural visions that we experience with our bodies.

16. Architecture embodies our bodies like a second skin.

17. Architecture is our interface to the external natural world.

18. Architecture is a fine art because it elevates the aesthetic sense in our lives.

19. The evoking of beauty is a central role of Architecture.

20. We exist because Architecture provides the ground for our existence.

2 ARCHITECTS

21.   Architects design buildings.

22.   Buildings are made up of materials arranged in space.

23.   Architects create Architecture by determining the forms of materials and arranging them in space.

24.   The arrangement of materials in space is composed construction.

25.   Constructions are physical or virtual.

26.   Both physical and virtual constructions are real.

27.   Physical constructions obey the immutable law of gravity and have to resist natural forces.

28.   Virtual constructions do not have to obey the law of gravity and certain natural forces.

29.   Buildings are physical constructions.

30.   Drawings and computer models are virtual constructions.

31. Architects design physical constructions through virtual constructions.

32. Architects also design physical constructions through analog physical constructions.

33. Analog physical constructions of architecture are physical scale models.

34. The virtual and analog constructions that architects create have to approximate the buildings that they precede.

35. Architects specify, within reasonable tolerances, most aspects of the designs that they create.

36. Architects seldom build buildings, but they should know how to build.

37. Architects are the stewards of how our built environments are shaped.

38. The public role of the architect is to advocate for the quality of our built environments.

39. Architects work with a team of professionals, who assist them with the various aspects of realizing their architectural designs.

40. The role of the architect is to provide leadership and coordination to the team of professionals who work on realizing an architectural design.

3 DESIGN

41.   Design allows us to change our present state to a preferred state.

42.   Design starts with the desire to change an existing state to a preferred state. This may be stated as a general design problem.

43.   Design progresses with a vague definition of a preferred state and follows a path of action to realize that preferred state.

44.   Design is not the solution to a single problem.

45.   Many interconnected problems have to be solved in the creation of a design.

46.   The solution of one problem in a design should not adversely affect the solution of another problem in the design.

47.   Keeping track of all the interconnected problems that affect each other in a design is a design skill.

48.   The main problem of Design is that the path of action to reach a preferred state from an existing state is usually

undetermined.

49. The task of Design is to determine the path of action from an existing state to a preferred state by making design decisions.

50. Designs belong to a time and a culture. They have a context.

51. Designs change in time and place to achieve similar preferred states.

52. Designs have to satisfy various performance criteria when they are realized.

53. The performance criteria for a design are pre-determined or emerge as the design process progresses.

54. The preferred state that a design should achieve is often arrived at through consensus in a social process.

55. The value of a design, except in meeting performance criteria, is determined through a political process.

56. Designs are often used as a precedent for subsequent designs, which are derived from them.

57. A design in a particular context may not be applicable or appropriate in a different context.

58. The creation of a design generates a unique body of knowledge that should be preserved as a cultural artifact.

59. Design knowledge combines knowledge from the two

cultures of Art and Science. Art enables life, and Science helps us understand it.

60.   Design allows us to shape our destiny.

4 FORM

61. Architectural form has to be imagined in the mind first.

62. Architectural forms come to our mind from the memories of architectural forms that we have experienced in our lives.

63. Architectural forms come to our mind through the manipulations of representational abstractions.

64. Architectural form has to be visualized and communicated.

65. Architectural forms are figural and legible.

66. Architectural forms always belong to, and are set apart from, a ground or context.

67. Architectural form gives shape to building materials.

68. Architectural form gives shape to the arrangement of building materials, which is their structure or composed construction.

69. Architectural form gives shape to the spaces that the arrangements of building materials define.

70.   Forms of materials have meaning.

71.   Forms of materials tell the story of their making.

72.   Forms of materials are derived from the technology used to make them.

73.   Some architectural forms that are envisioned drive the invention of technologies to make them.

74.   Sometimes the architectural forms come first, sometimes the technology used to make them comes first.

75.   Forms belong to a time and a culture. They have a context.

76.   Some forms are universal and transcend time and culture.

77.   Forms have a major influence on the performance of designs that are derived from them.

78.   Sometimes all is won or lost when an architectural form is first imagined.

79.   An architectural form evolves from the realm of the intangible to the realm of the tangible.

80.   Perceiving an architectural form in a work of Architecture is a skill that has to be acquired.

5 MATERIALS

81.   Architectural materials have properties.

82.   Properties of architectural materials are both external and intrinsic.

83.   External properties of architectural materials are color and texture.

84.   The color and texture of architectural materials are perceived as light evokes them.

85.   Light changes throughout the day and the seasons.

86.   Perception of the external property of an architectural material is ephemeral.

87.   Intrinsic properties of architectural materials are weight and strength.

88.   Weight and strength are perceived through a kinesthetic sense.

89.   Perception of an intrinsic property of an architectural material is more enduring.

90. Architectural materials have a natural form.

91. The natural form of materials is transformed by architects into architectural form through design.

92. Technologies of manufacturing allow architects to transform the natural forms of materials into architectural forms.

93. Architects have to give materials architectural form such that the materials can be transformed into them from their natural state.

94. The transformation of materials from their natural form to architectural forms requires energy.

95. Architectural ethics aims to reduce the energy used to transform materials from their natural form to architectural forms.

96. Architectural ethics aims to use materials that are renewable and whose supply can be sustained.

97. Architectural materials found in a locale are often the most appropriate for use in creating an architectural design at that location.

98. Architectural materials determine the performance of the architectural designs created with them.

99. The most crucial properties of architectural materials that influence their environmental performance are their surface properties.

100. Architectural materials are used by architects to evoke immaterial experiences.

6 REPRESENTATION

101. Architectural form is realized through drawing, computational modeling, and making.

102. Drawing, computational modeling, and making are controlled by conventions.

103. Orthographic, axonometric, and perspective projections are conventions of drawing.

104. Computational abstractions are conventions of computational modeling.

105. Cutting, joining, carving, folding, casting, weaving, and stitching are conventions of making.

106. The conventions of representations often restrict the designs that architects create.

107. The processes of drawing, computational modeling, and making happen in the world of representations.

108. The fidelity of the representation to the imagined architectural form is of great value in Architecture.

109. Architects use their representations as a vehicle for

thinking about their design.

110. Each architectural representation has an insight that it affords. It provides a particular viewpoint.

111. Certain types of thinking are associated with certain types of architectural representations.

112. Architectural representations are a means to solve design problems.

113. The conventions of architectural representations often drive the architectural forms that architects imagine and design.

114. We often end up dwelling in Architecture that is created based on the conventions of architectural representations.

115. Simulations are a powerful form of representation used by architects.

116. Architectural simulations show how a design would perform if built.

117. Architectural simulations are only approximations of the real experiences a design would provide if built.

118. Sometimes a simulation is all that is created for an architectural design and is preserved as a cultural artifact.

119. The effectiveness of an architectural simulation depends on how closely it matches the reality it is trying to simulate.

120. The language of simulations is often embedded in the
     languages of Science, or systems of knowledge.

7 EXPERIENCE

121. Architecture is experienced by many people.

122. Each person brings their own conditioning to the experience of Architecture.

123. Everyone experiences Architecture in their own way.

124. An architect cannot control all the ways in which his or her design is experienced.

125. An architect tries to anticipate all the experiences that his or her design can afford.

126. An experienced architect is very rich in his or her anticipations of how a design can be experienced.

127. Architectural experience is not confined to the experience of materials and their arrangement in space.

128. Forms of materials and their spatial arrangement communicate other ideas.

129. Architecture *informs*.

130. The production and consumption of architectural forms

as experience is a cultural activity.

131.   Spatial arrangements of materials create the stages for life to unfold.

132.   Architectural designs suggest possibilities for action. You may walk down a path, climb some stairs, or sit on a ledge.

133.   Architecture enables life, its actions, and experiences.

134.   Architectural experience is part of our cultural memory.

135.   Architectural experiences leave neural traces in our minds that shape how we anticipate future experiences.

136.   A lot of what we experience in life is determined by the Architecture in which we are situated.

137.   Our lives are conditioned by our architectural experiences.

138.   Architecture offers the possibility of creating new experiences in our lives that we have not experienced before.

139.   Not all architectural experiences are beneficial to us. Some architectural experiences can selectively harm individuals.

140.   Architectural experiences should be enabled for the greatest possible good for the most number of people.

8 VALUE

141. Works of Architecture are created amidst other works of Architecture.

142. Relationships between works of Architecture created at different times enable the fabric of history to be woven.

143. A place is a meaningful experience of a particular arrangement of materials in space.

144. Places are what are remembered in Architecture.

145. You go to various places in your lives, not to arrangements of materials in space.

146. A place has its own *genius loci* or spirit of place.

147. The experience of a place can be spiritual. It can transcend our senses.

148. Places and spaces organize our lives.

149. Existence as *ex sistare* is possible only when you can stand out in a figural sense.

150. Architecture enables life to stand out as a meaningful

experience.

151. To go from here to there in our lives, we need a 'here' and a 'there.' Architecture provides the 'here' and 'there.'

152. Architecture is the ground of existence.

153. The value of a work of Architecture is determined through a social process that involves lay people, educators, critics, social leaders, and even clergy.

154. A major concern of architects is that the value of a work of Architecture is often determined through a political process.

155. What is valued as good Architecture changes from time to time, as people's needs and minds change.

156. The value of a work of Architecture is not commensurate with the money spent on creating the work.

157. The value of a work of Architecture is determined by the richness of lives that it enables.

158. The value of a work of Architecture is determined by its sustainability.

159. Because a work of Architecture arises in a particular time and in a particular place, it has value as a provider of cultural identity.

160. All Architecture has the intrinsic value of enabling lives, mainly for the better, sometimes for the worse.

9 SPACE AND TIME

161.   Time is marked by changing space.

162.   We know of an architectural space as belonging to the particular time when its perception was enabled.

163.   Architecture endures as Time passes.

164.   We can build a record of Time only through a changing physical state, which is our Architecture.

165.   Forms occupy space and are distributed in space.

166.   Forms define a space that is experienced.

167.   Natural space is the *sine qua non* of all existence.

168.   Architectural space is a component of natural space.

169.   Architectural space has to be visualized and communicated.

170.   Architectural space is defined by conventions.

171.   A Cartesian universal grid in three dimensions is one convention to define architectural space.

172. Space is defined by activities that *take (possession of) place*.

173. Space is defined by perceived boundaries.

174. Spatial boundaries change for each experiencing individual.

175. Spatial boundaries change with a change in our location

176. All of us cannot experience the same space from the same viewpoint at once.

177. The boundaries of space are also the edges of materials.

178. When architects shape spaces, they are also deciding the edges of materials and their arrangement in space.

179. In architectural design, there is a constant going back and forth between the edges of materials and the boundaries of space.

180. The perceptual qualities of spaces change in time, during the day, and in the seasons.

181. Our experience of a space is ephemeral but real.

182. Architects do not create space; they enable the experience of a space by the perceiving inhabitants of the space.

183. Space slices Time, and Time slices Space.

10 RUINS

184. Buildings die.

185. Dead buildings have been buried alive.

186. Dead buildings left standing are ruins.

187. Architectural ruins connect us to the past through traces of memory.

188. Architectural ruins are of another time.

189. Architectural ruins allow us to travel back in time.

190. Architectural ruins disturb the clock of the present by triggering our memories.

191. The traces of architectural ruins are built lessons.

192. One can learn a lot from architectural ruins if one knows how to read them.

193. We need architectural ruins to remind us where we have been.

194. Architectural ruins may allow us to recapture Time.

195.   Buildings, like living things, need to be preserved.

196.   A subtlety that is preserved in an architectural ruin is the original architectural form. This allows architectural ideas to live on.

197.   Architectural ruins can be revived into rebirth by building on them.

198.   When we build anew on architectural ruins, we create integrated layers of Space and Time that rewrite their history.

199.   Ruins act to preserve cultural identity.

200.   All Architecture eventually ends in ruins.

ABOUT THE AUTHOR

An architect by education and training, Ganapathy Mahalingam completed an undergraduate professional education in Architecture at the School of Architecture and Planning in Chennai, India, and became a registered architect in 1984. Ganapathy came to the United States in 1985 to pursue a Master's degree in Architecture, which he earned at Iowa State University in 1986. He taught computer-aided design at Iowa State University for a year before he returned to India to practice Architecture. Ganapathy came back to the United States to complete a Ph.D. in Architecture at the University of Florida, which was awarded in 1995. Having spent half of his life in the culture of India and half of his life in the culture of the United States, he has that balanced experience in life that spans the Old World and the New World. Currently educating future generations of architects at North Dakota State University, he is seeking to share...in the words of Le Corbusier...*les carnets de la recherché patiente...*

Made in the USA
Monee, IL
08 July 2026

56679418R00017